A Little English City
A photographic documentary
of the Lancaster and Morecambe district

D J Clark

Foreword by
Bryan Carter

NEXTNORTH

A Little English City

dedicated to Mary

A Little English City
Foreword
by Bryan Carter

In Year 2000 Lancaster stood at a painful crossroads in its long and varied history. Long gone were the often modest but measured economic certainties of its recent past. Instead our wonderful, and in parts picturesque, Little English City and its beautiful environs were seeking a new purpose and future.

It would be facile and dishonest to suggest that a rosy future was guaranteed. How was a small town, which almost accidentally won city status as a Coronation Day gesture by King George VI in 1937, to compete in global markets? Remember that at the end of the last millennium the area served by Lancaster City Council took in the jaded, faded and problem-ridden nearby resort of Morecambe and the old railway town of Carnforth. There was much of the lush Lune Valley and Glasson Dock and Heysham with their harbours on south and north sides of the River Lune. Considerable acreage of land north of the River Wyre also fell within the City Council area as well as Lancaster itself. D.J.Clark has captured the diversity of character of the area in his pictures.

More than 130,000 souls lived in the City Council area at the end of the second millennium. Their number was growing fast. By year 2006, the population was expected to grow by 14,600 to 147,000. Within that cold statistic lay a challenging range of social issues - some of

Start of the Galgate Duck Race.

local origin, some reflecting national trends - which had to be addressed in tandem with creating a new economic infrastructure. In the decade to 2006, the number of entrants to the labour market was growing at twice the rate elsewhere in the county. They needed jobs. A bigger population also had to have more homes, its children wanted schools and all age groups sought leisure facilities, whether publicly or commercially provided. How were workplaces and housing to be created without adding to already considerable pressures on the local environment? And how were long established and at times failing communities to be rebuilt?

The social mix in Lancaster itself was fast changing taking in long-distance commuters to other Lancashire towns, living in what to locals were hugely expensive properties - up to £350,000 - on new estates on the edge of the city. But Government statisticians had also identified certain riverside areas in Lancaster and parts of Morecambe as having some of the worst social problems in the country. It is not glib to borrow from Dickens to suggest that it was almost a tale of two cities.

Young boys cut through an alley between Dallas Road and Fenton Street, Lancaster, on the way to Mosque.

. . . the enormity of the task of those who shape our lives -

Therein lay the enormity of the task of those who shape our lives - to seek to provide a future of equality of opportunity for all. It is not Utopian socialist thinking to regard a society characterised by a wide gulf between the "haves" and "have-nots" as unhealthy. In doing little to address that division, we sow the seeds of even bigger future social ills. Many considered Lancaster vibrant and exciting despite its economic travails. But the rose-tinted view had to be balanced with a more sober assessment taking in some of the painful realities.

Final whistle, England v Germany at the Friary and Firkin pub, Lancaster.

debut on local streets. Alcohol-fuelled violence, especially at weekends, was a major problem for the police after the opening of new clubs and pubs with a combined capacity of more than 4,000 in recent times. Many older people rightly or wrongly perceived the city centre as off-limits after dark. Quite how a monstrous six-screen cinema under construction on a wholly inappropriate site, in a wholly inappropriate style, would fare remained to be seen.

Some once-proud inter-war estates, built by the Council at a time when housing was seen as a community responsibility, have degenerated into "sinks". They absorbed the human debris of the Thatcher-inspired notion that there was no such thing as society, that market forces were always right, that if the pig with the biggest snout emptied the trough, then tough on the rest.

day to day life for many Lancastrians with traditional feasts and

festivities marking high points in the year by year routine.

Lancaster - and Morecambe - had deep-seated drug cultures with hard and soft drugs in social and addictive use. Crack cocaine had recently made its

On a millennial scale, beggars on the streets of Lancaster were a recent phenomenon. Although highly visible and by now part of the street furniture, they were not typical. As D.J.Clark's portfolio so vividly illustrates, day to day life still went on for many Lancastrians with traditional feasts and festivities marking high points in the year by year routine. A quick check on the local newspaper - the Lancaster Guardian, founded 1837 - similarly revealed a rich collection of people-oriented tales but none millennial in importance. A local actress who had become a national television star. A landlord vanished with his pub's £70,000 Christmas Club savings. Older folks mourned the death of a Lancaster girl who became Miss World as a teenager in the 1960s.

High technology may have been taking over the workplace but as the Clark pictures show, babies were still christened. Parents complained that their children were addicted to computer games, but many lads still didn't mind a bloody nose playing winter rugby at school. Marriage was no longer a pre-requisite for man and woman to live together. But when a couple decided to formally tie the knot a bit of show - like the stretch limousine on the council estate - was often the order of

the day, and a chance for the little girl to dress up in the bridesmaid's finery. And not far from power stations churning out nuclear-generated electricity at Heysham, fishermen and women still used centuries-old techniques to reap the harvest of the Lune.

The Clark portfolio also reminds us of the 2,000-year history of our town or city. The majestic Castle, parts of which are believed to date back 1,000 years, was built on the site of the Roman fort which marked the birth of Lancaster. Next door, the main area of the Priory dates back to 1430. In the Middle Ages Lancaster was a small market town - Charter granted in 1292 - serving the local hinterland. At the end of the last

Charlotte looks on as Cawthorne's Endowed School perform *A Mid Summer Nights Dream* at the Abbeystead Pageant.

millennium, much of the Castle, which should have been a prime tourism asset, was used as a prison. It had also served as administrative headquarters for Lancashire into the 19th century.

For decades the world bought linoleum and oilcloth made in Lancaster by the firms of Williamson and Storey.

The Castle looks down on St George's Quay from which local shipping traded with America and the West Indies in the golden years of Lancaster as a port in the sail powered days of the 18th century. In 1799 alone, goods then worth £2.5m left Lancaster, but competition from Liverpool and the advent of ever bigger ships, which were unable to navigate the Lune, meant an end to the glory days. But still the population grew from 9,000 to 40,000 in the 19th century. For decades late in that period and well into mid-20th century the world bought linoleum and oilcloth made in Lancaster by the firms of Williamson and Storey. Both have changed hands several times in recent years and no longer bear the names of the founding dynasties. What was Williamson's is now effectively German-owned while Americans control the fate of the former Storey operation. Businesses that once employed more than 6,000 now provide work for about a tenth that figure. And therein lies the core of Lancaster's economic malaise. Those jobs lost to major de-industrialisation in the 1970s and 1980s have never been effectively replaced. Manufacturing which once dominated the district had declined so that it made up only 12.4 per cent of total employment at the end of the last millennium. More than 80 per cent of all jobs outside agriculture lay in the service sector. Our biggest employers were in the public sector or began life on the back of public money.

Lancaster University, founded in 1964 and located on a huge site just outside the city, had 10,000

View of the City beyond the Cathedral.

registered students and 2,000 staff, full and part-time, academic and non-academic. St Martin's College no longer exclusively trained teachers, rather concentrating on health education. At time of writing the University looked set for major new Government funding aimed at using Lancaster research to help create new Lancaster businesses and nurture existing firms.

Closure of the Moor and Royal Albert psychiatric hospitals, which at their peak housed 4,000 patients, has also taken a toll on local job opportunities. The two Heysham power stations began life in public ownership but, became privately run and saw their combined workforce cut to around 1,000.

The Castle and the city's second prison - the Young Offenders' Institution known locally as "The Farms" - provided work for several hundred. For the unqualified, unskilled or untrained, employment opportunities were, however, limited. Hence the huge range of training courses on offer in a bid to help curb the numbers of state benefit claimants and provide a skilled workforce for inward investors willing to move

into the area. But that was only part of the problem.

On a national scale, another legacy of the Thatcher years was the emphatic centralisation of government, although recent years had seen some shift towards regionalism. Purely local authorities were but bit players, especially relatively small bodies like Lancaster City Council.

Lancaster University graduation ceremony.

In the Town Hall a woefully under-resourced Economic Development Department struggled valiantly to help attract job providers to the district. But ever more key decisions on vital funding were made regionally, nationally, even internationally. Our Little English City had to compete in the big league, fighting giants like Manchester and Liverpool for available money.

Peripatetic Promenaders perform in Sun Street Square, Lancaster.

A report from the Economic Development Department warned: "The economic future of Lancaster District cannot be separated from the condition and well being of the wider economy and the ability of the area to take advantage of policies and initiatives at a European, national and regional level." Success had been limited. Under various guises, cash was being made available by both UK government and the European Union to help rebuild Lancaster and environs. But the availability of cash offered no guarantees. New business had to be attracted from outside or generated locally and that was proving difficult in the light of core problems.

Industrial land with all necessary services laid on was in short supply. Development acreage was largely focused in the Heysham area but road links to it were congested and rail freight schedules non-existent. Years of campaigning for a new road from the M6 motorway to Heysham had proved unsuccessful. A simple accident or small section of carriageway repairs often produced wide-ranging gridlock in the city. If late for an appointment, one simply muttered "traffic" and all was forgiven.

Quality office space suitable for technology-based businesses was in ultra short supply. There was an easily identified lack of vision among the local politicians of the Morecambe Bay Independents who controlled the affairs of Lancaster City Council with a minority administration. They grandly talked of turning the dog-eared detritus of decades of decay in Morecambe into an upmarket Lake District-style resort. No costing or a positive plan, just words.

Lancaster itself did not even benefit from that level of attention. One proposal was to sell the city's publicly owned 200-year-old Museum. The notion was rejected after a wave of public outrage. If tourism was to be a staple industry of the future where was the logic in selling off key historic assets like

the City Museum - a magnificent

structure completed in 1783 in the golden years of our city as a port. It was one of a small number of notable landmarks in a city centre becoming characterised by branches of High Street multiple shopping chains. Of the small independent local trader there was but little remaining evidence.

All was not gloom however. So far, this brief essay has mused on history and economy with a seasoning of politics. Many of the Clark pictures are about people, young and old, professional and those who used to be termed working class, advantaged and disadvantaged, urban and rural alike. They show our demographically changing community at work and

Breaktime,
Central Lancaster High School.

. . . people, young and old, professional and those who used to

be termed working class, advantaged and disadvantaged, urban and rural alike.

play. City schools still enjoyed a reputation envied elsewhere and added weight to the "tale of two cities" argument. Grammar schools for boys and girls had survived politically inspired reorganisations that elsewhere saw an end to selection at age 11. For the boys Lancaster Royal Grammar School has its roots in the 13th century. Annually it sent small armies of young adults replete with myriad A levels to Oxford and Cambridge. Headmaster Peter Mawby, who retired in 2001, ruefully pointed out that few of his past pupils returned to build their adult lives here because work opportunities were so limited. Lancaster Girls Grammar "only" goes back to 1907 but

Easter Field Football Competition, Giant Axe, Lancaster.

enjoyed an excellent reputation. Across the district some other comprehensive secondary education establishments looked enviously at facilities and funding available to the grammar schools. Primary schools ranged from those serving comfortable middle class areas to those where teachers were as much skilled social workers as educators in dealing with the problems of multiple-deprivation in parts of both Lancaster and Morecambe.

Hospital facilities were widely regarded as good with Royal Lancaster Infirmary serving a wide local area. Motorway and ever-more costly rail services provided links to north and south. Heysham offered ferry links to the Isle of Man and Ireland for both passengers and freight.

Social life in Lancaster was rooted in tradition but at the same time was changing to meet new tastes. Amateur sport

few who daily crossed Skerton Bridge paused to consider

the marvels of a structure dating back to the era of the horse and cart.

was strong. Football, rugby union and league, golf, rowing, cricket, tennis, bowling, swimming were all well established with good facilities. City and resort both had semi-professional soccer teams. In 2000 Lancaster City FC won the biggest cup final in its 95-year history, beating Worksop Town 1-0 for the Unibond League Challenge Cup. Morecambe reached the third round of the FA Cup with a 2-1 win over Nationwide League Cambridge United. It was no mean achievement.

Amateur theatre and music thrived. Lancaster Choral Society was still going strong, having given its first public concert in the Grand Theatre - then the Athenaeum - back in 1836. The Lancaster Red Rose Amateur Operatic and Dramatic Society was founded in 1935. The Haffner Orchestra, founded in 1977, had about 40 playing members.

Lancaster always had strong and continuing links with the Army, perhaps because it has proved fertile recruiting ground in times of unemployment. The connection began in 1881 when the King's Own Royal

social life in Lancaster was rooted in tradition but at the same time was changing to meet new tastes

Skerton Bridge

Lancaster Regiment moved into the newly-built Bowerham Barracks, which is now part of St Martin's College. Amalgamations have seen the name changed to the King's Own Royal Border Regiment, but it is still very much Lancaster's "King's Own" for locals.

Lancaster had always been a hard-drinking town

economy, architecture, political institutions are not what makes a community. The core ingredient at any time in history is people

and until fairly recently had two small local breweries. Ale was however no longer brewed in the city. Much of that consumed at the end of the last millennium bore the name of nationally promoted brands, many of them foul and gassy apologies for decent beer. The younger element in our community - and from many other parts of the North West - seemed to feel a manic urge to congregate in dark establishments where conversation was impossible because of multi-decibel so-called "music." Price competition was forcing ever

Railings on the road to Heysham harbour and power stations.

more small, traditional pubs into closure or revamping in a more "modern" image. Some things and some elements of the cityscape could not be changed however. We had numerous architectural and engineering gems locally. Few who daily crossed Skerton Bridge paused to consider the marvels of a structure dating back to 1788 and the era of the horse and cart. It had become a focal point of Lancaster's notorious one-way traffic system. The Custom House on the Quay was completed in 1764 to a design by Richard Gillow of the world-renowned cabinet making family, who so long graced Lancaster. Alas no more.

John Rennie's 1797 Aqueduct carrying the canal across the Lune 50 feet below was another oft-forgotten treasure, a masterpiece of British civil engineering history. But economy, architecture, political institutions are not what makes a community. The core ingredient at any time in history is people. It is that fact which D.J.Clark's pictures celebrate.

Dear reader - do not be downhearted by this essay. As a native-born Lancastrian, I love this city. I have invested much of my life and career in it. I claim the right to tell an honest story in service of the city.

The end of the last millennium undoubtedly marked difficult times. We had been there before. We would be there again. But Lancaster would survive and hopefully prosper again.

Change in the hi-tech world was however rapid and comprehensive. Only a brave man would forecast what our Little English City would look like in Year 3000. As MP Hilton Dawson - North East born but celebrating 20 years as a city resident - remarked:

"It is awesome to contemplate the next 1,000 years in Lancaster."

Guy Fawkes Fireworks explode over the nearly-finished Millennium Bridge.

Trevor Hawkin of "URBAN1",
Lancaster's elite binmen crew,
clearing Scotforth South.

Up before daybreak, papergirl
Anne-Marie crosses Caton Road
to deliver to the Lansil Industrial
Estate.

Returning from a nightshift, District Nurse Louise Yates prepares her five sons for school and nursery. Yealand Drive, Lancaster.

With their three daughters out
playing, Jason Mooney and partner
Lorraine Clark "stop in".
Ryelands Estate.

Prize winners of a book character
competition parade at morning
assembly.
Christ Church School, Carnforth.

Year nine P.E. Class.
Central Lancaster High School.

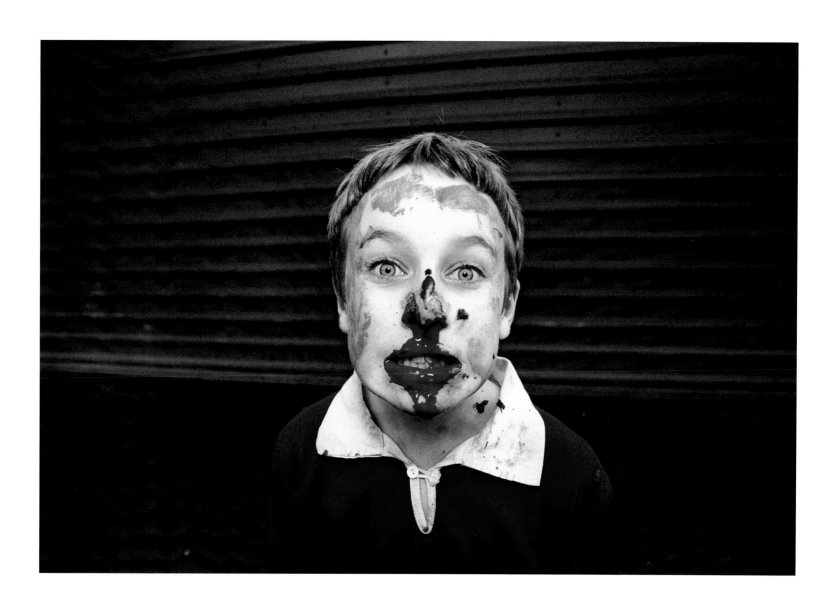

Remarkably unconcerned about
his rugby injury, year seven pupil
Sam poses for the camera.
Lancaster Royal Grammar School.

Sarah, a creative arts student, develops her own visual studio as part of a drama project. Beaumont College, Lancaster.

Fine art student Liz Smith works in St.Martin's College studio.

'A' Level art practicals.
Lancaster Royal Grammar School
and Lancaster Girls Grammar School.

Martin Higginson, managing director of new media company, Telezones. Church Street, Lancaster.

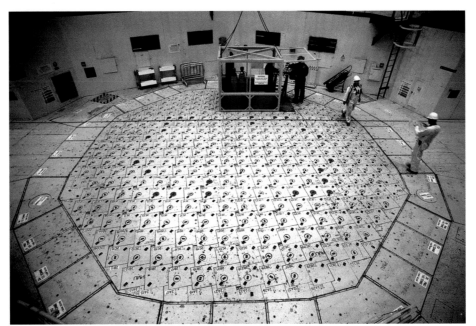

On top of a reactor, Heysham I nuclear Power Station.

Design meeting at Reebock.
Moorgate, Lancaster.

Pickers, Reebok warehouse.
White Lund Industrial Estate.

Old Lancaster Bus Station.
A new one opened March 2001.

Frontierland, to be developed as a factory outlet shopping centre. Morecambe.

Known to his workmates as "Pornstar", bricklayer Trevor Newsham plays for the camera. Crofter's Fold, Galgate.

The new mill, Pye Farm Feeds,
Lansil Industrial Estate.

The Ruskin Centre,
Lancaster University.

Refurbished from its medieval past, Lancaster Castle continues to serve as a prison.

Castle spirits and spooks mysteriously interfere with pictures taken inside, producing strange colour effects.

In spite of the cramped conditions and thick stone walls, it is generally liked by the inmates who refer to it as a friendly jail.

Paul looks into camera as Police
Constable Tim Dodgson discusses
safe use of fireworks. On the beat,
Ridge Estate, Lancaster.

Blades Street playground,
Lancaster.

"Odd", as he is known to his
friends, shows off a facial tattoo.

The homeless and travellers meet to drink and socialise in Dalton Square.

Big Issue seller,
Joanna Midnight Jones.
Market Street, Lancaster.
She died March 29th 2001.

Dinner on the prom,
Morecambe.

Market seller Lynne Austin,
Assembly Rooms Market, Lancaster.

Lancaster indoor market.

Lancaster Auction Mart.

Lost in The Maze,
Morecambe Stone Jetty.

Staircase, Midland Hotel,
Morecambe.

Eric Morecambe statue,
Morecambe prom.

Determined to be the first person to cross the new cycle bridge, worker Gerard McGowen crosses on his daughter's bike as the first section is lowered into place.

Billy Davidson the crane assistant, checks the rigging from the man rider.

Henry Birkett, sheep farmer,
Overton.

Farmer's son Henry assists in fixing a quad bike puncture. Over Wyresdale.

Under threat of political intervention,
hounds turn up to the Boxing Day
hunt.

Lancaster/Forton Services,
M6 motorway.

Heysham Nuclear Power Stations.

Trevor Owen shoots the net just
off Abbey Light, Lune Estuary.

Driftnet fisherman Tom Smith still
prefers to use a sail. Lune Estuary.

Morecambe beach.

St. Patrick's Chapel, Heysham Head.

Cedric Robinson, former Queen's
Guide, leads walkers across
Morecambe Bay.

Fireworks light up the Bay for
the grand finale of Morecambe's
Festival of Water and Light.

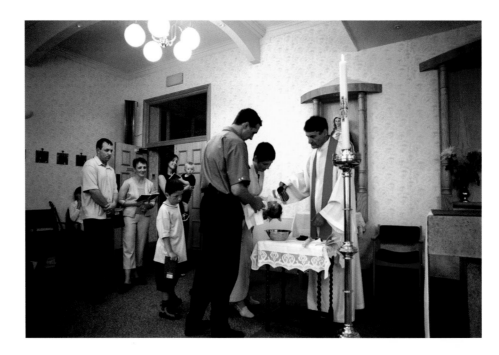

The Christening of Ellie.
Nazareth House Chapel,
Lancaster.

Natasha cuts her First Communion
cake, St.Bernadette's Church.

Amy, Dolphinholme's newly crowned Rose Queen, makes her first speech at the Field Day as Master of Ceremonies Allen Norris leaves the stage.

Bridesmaids Leann and Chantelle prepare for their sisters wedding. Mount Avenue, Skerton.

Early, best man Mark and groom Martin wait for the limousine chauffeur to prepare the car for the short drive to the church. Mainway Flats, Skerton.

Bridesmaids Chantelle and Naomi rush ahead of the bride and groom to throw confetti as they leave the church grounds. St. Josephs Church, Skerton.

Changed out of her dress, bride Lisa takes a break from the dance floor. The Phoenix Club, Lancaster.

On a day of visits to homes for
the elderly, Lancaster City Mayor
Edna Jones talks with Marjorie
Thompson at Moor Platt Home
for the Elderly, Caton.

Resident at Nazareth House
Nursing Home, Lancaster.

Planning meeting,
Cathedral House, Lancaster.

Mourners visit the Bishops Lying
in State, Lancaster Cathedral.

People of Morecambe pay tribute to those who gave
their lives in war.

Good Friday at Williamson Park.

Morning service at St.Thomas
Church, Lancaster.

Fancy dress competitor at the
Galgate Gala.

Millennium Street Party,
Princess Avenue, Lancaster.

Tide and Time festival,
Crook O' Lune, Caton.

Sunday afternoon, Arnside.

Photographer George Coupe
takes press pictures at the dress
rehearsal of the Duke's Playhouse
production of   *Don Quixote*,
Williamson Park, Lancaster.

Pete Moser leads Bay Beat Street
Band at Morecambe's *Tide and
Time Festival.*

England beat Germany, Euro 2000,
Friary and Firkin pub, Lancaster.

Morecambe beat Cambridge United in the second round of the FA Cup. Christie Park, Morecambe.

The Doyle household
7a.m. Christmas morning,
Scotforth, Lancaster.

The Craig household "Christmas
Dinner". Freehold, Lancaster.

Graduation Ball,
Lancaster University.

Leighton Hall, *Last Night of the Proms*. Yealand Redmayne, near Carnforth.

Holidays in the Sun punk festival
at the Dome, Morecambe.

Liquid Night Club charity fashion
show, Lancaster.

New Year celebrations,
Liquid Night Club, Lancaster.

Lancaster Footlights' Christmas
pantomime *Mother Goose* at
the Grand Theatre.